Danny's Diary

Susan Jayne Rose

To my wonderful son Daniel. You are, and always will be, my best work.

Also to Matty my gorgeous grandson
who has brought sunshine to my world.

Love you both to the moon and back.

Danny's Diary

November 19th

It was just an ordinary day. Was walking home from school with my best friend Joy from next door. Autumn is my favourite time of year. We came back through the park collecting shiny conkers on our way, kicking up the leaves like we always did.

We've been friends for as long as I can remember. To be honest we're more like family. Mom once said to me that there all kinds of families. Ours is the best! Joy and her mom moved in when her mom and dad divorced. We've been on holidays together and had some great days out too. There are five of us when we go out: me, Mom, Joy, her mom and her grandad.

We were chatting about the day's events as usual: about how boring Mr. Atkins is in ICT, how brilliant our team was at winning the basketball match in P.E. and how lucky we are to have Mrs. Hart for our last year in Juniors. She's one of those teachers that inspire you to be the best you can be. Before we knew it, we were at our front doors. Joy did her routine rummaging for her keys. Don't know why. They are always right at the very bottom. I grabbed mine from my pocket and turned the key in my front door.

Patch came bounding up to lick my hand. She's always so excited to see me. Since she came to live with us three years ago we have become inseparable. She always knows how I'm feeling and when she looks at me with her big brown eyes it's like she understands every word I say – and every word I <u>don't</u> say.

I love our house. Always like the way the sun shines through the stained glass in the front door. When I am inside, it makes patterns on the lounge carpet. Kings Road is a handy place to live. There are shops across the road, a park nearby and it's only a short walk to school.

That's weird, no radio. Mom always had that on. I shouted "Hi Mom, I'm home!" She was upstairs and shouted down in a voice that seemed to have an edge to it: "Hello love, don't put the TV on, I need to talk to you. I'll be down in a minute." What's that about? I wondered. She'd probably peeped round my door and seen the state of my bedroom. Launched myself onto the settee and sank into the deep cushions.

I waited.

Looking round the room, I noticed Mom had moved the photos on the fire surround. The one of me and her had been put next to the one of me, Mom and Nan. She'd probably been dusting. Our surround is, in my opinion, quite unique. It has pieces of unusual crystals, shells from various holidays, a box of feathers, candles and a small blue vase full of wild flowers. I once asked Mom why she had a box of feathers. She said: "I find when angels are near, feathers appear. They give you comfort, encouragement, love, guidance and protection from afar. Sometimes I pick them up, but not always. You don't have to." I remember thinking, what a nice thought, but I don't really believe it. If it helps her, that's fine.

My Mom's books lay on the coffee table: one on complementary therapies (whatever those are), one on Angels and one on gardening. My friends Stu and Lee who are brothers think Mom's unusual! I think she's just different and I like that. Different means unique. A small pair of white angel wings made from feathers hang from the corner of the large mirror. Gold thread binds them together. Strange what you really look at when there's no TV on...

Where was Mom and what was taking so long?

At last I heard footsteps on the stairs and Mom came into the lounge. She sat down next to me on the settee and hugged me, tighter than was usual, I thought. Patch put a paw on Mom's knee. She usually only does that when there's something wrong. My heart beat faster. When I looked closely at Mom, she was red-eyed and pale. "I've got something to tell you, Danny," and then she hesitated. My mind was racing, my heart thumping. Was she ill? Her voice trembling, she spoke in almost a whisper, saying "Danny, I'm so sorry, your Nan's gone." Gone where, I thought? She can't mean... Mom said: "After you'd gone to school I took a cup of tea up to her and I couldn't wake her."

I froze, stared at the window, and as her hand reached for mine I heard soft sobs. After what seemed like ages I realised they were mine. I thought my heart would break. My Nan was a huge part of my life: my friend, my ally and the one I told my secrets to. This can't be happening – it's not true. I know old people don't live forever, I just never thought about it. Why would I? I'm just a kid.

My world stood still. Mom was saying something but I

couldn't hear her. What were we both going to do now? I wanted to rewind and go back to half an hour before in the park. Everything had been OK then. Just then Patch jumped up on the settee beside me. Mom doesn't normally allow that but she didn't say anything.

November 20th

Mom said I didn't have to go to school today so I went back to bed with my cornflakes and toast. I didn't really feel like eating but I was hungry. Patch was beside me. We watched TV but didn't really know what was on. Opened the curtains. The sky was grey like my mood. My head felt foggy. Yesterday was unreal. Could hear Mom on the phone - couldn't hear what she was saying though. Heard the phone ring several times. Guess Mom was talking to friends about Nan.

Eventually I plodded down the stairs and flopped onto the settee. Mom was sitting holding a mug of tea. She asked how I'd slept and I asked her. Both of us badly of course. She ruffled my hair, patted my shoulder and went to the kitchen. The day passed in a bit of a blur really. I didn't even get out of my pj's all day.

Normally Mom would have gone mad, but not today.

November 21st

I decided to go into school though Mom said "No pressure, love." Thought a bit of a normal routine might help. Called for Joy and she hugged me without saying anything. We set off early as we often dawdle in the mornings. I certainly wasn't in any rush today, that's for sure. Joy asked me how I was feeling. I said numb. She told me how she'd felt when her Nanny died. And her hamster. Funny, it was quite similar! Wonder if Nan would mind being compared to a pet?

November 22nd

I usually love the weekends but it was going to be different now. Most Saturdays we'd take Nan out somewhere, go for lunch then back home for tea and board games. Wondered what we'd do now. Mom asked me to think about if I want to go to the funeral. She said it was up to me. I told her straight away I didn't want to. If I go, that will make it real. She said she understood. I knew it was too hard for me to face. Mom took me to the safari park. Nan had given Mom a voucher for her birthday and it was about to run out, so even though we didn't feel like it we felt we should go.

We both made an effort to enjoy ourselves but it was weird.

November 26th

When I got home from school Mom had several vases of flowers in the lounge and more sympathy cards had arrived. I didn't read any of them – didn't want to – but Mom said they were for both of us. Mom was quieter than usual. Guess it's because it's the funeral tomorrow.

Mom said that her best friend Chris had been round for the day. She said that had helped as Chris was very supportive.

We'd chosen the funeral flowers together and they would be coming in the morning, thankfully after I'd gone to school. Mom had chosen purple and white flowers – Nan's favourite – and Mom had let me choose my own. I'd chosen all kinds of purple and white wild flowers. The man was going to put them in the shape of the letters saying 'Nan'.

November 27th

Worst day of my life. Felt guilty not going with Mom but she said "It's OK. I have my friends there for support. You must do what you feel. Everyone's different. There's no right or wrong way."

Didn't hear any of the lessons today. Was in a world of my own. It rained all day. I sat by the window and counted raindrops. The sky was grey. The clouds were grey. I was grey. I could cry now but I'm holding back because if I start I think I might drown. Mrs. Hart was thoughtful though. She said "I know this is a difficult day for you, so if you want to talk I'll be in my office break time and lunch time, so just come and find me."

The clock went round slowly and the day dragged.

Joy and I ambled slowly home. Didn't want to hear about Mom's day so was in no hurry. Joy was thoughtful and said: "We don't have to talk unless you want to." I said: "I don't, thanks." She grabbed hold of my hand and squeezed it tightly, just for a second. "I like your hands, Danny, they're big and strong and make me feel safe." That's funny, Nan used to say that as well. Unexpectedly as we turned into our road the rain stopped and a rainbow appeared just in front of us. Just for a moment my mood lifted.

Mom and I didn't talk about the day. She knew I'd ask when I was ready. We had a hug and a cry and I said "I know it's been a horrible day for you Mom. Love you." Patch and I went in the garden. She didn't want to play ball so we just sat together. It was a bit wet and cold but the sun had come out.

December 1st

There's Christmas everywhere but I'm not really in the mood. We'd usually have our tree up today but Mom didn't mention it and neither did I.

Nan moved in with us last year after Poppa died but Mom and I had not been in her room since she'd gone. I decided to take a look while Mom was in the shower. My hand trembled on the wooden doorknob and my heart pounded as I opened the door just a bit. I half expected my Nan to be there. I know she's gone but I just can't believe it yet. I was glad I had Patch with me. I don't know why I felt weird about going in there. Anyway we went in and I sat in her chair by the window. She loved watching the birds feed and the changing seasons, especially the colours of autumn. Patch went and rested her head on Nan's bed, just like she'd always done when Nan was there. I hadn't thought about how much Patch must be missing her as well.

I felt OK. Hugging her purple scarf, I was comforted by her perfume. Mom used to say to her: "Why don't you wear it every day. It's your favourite." She'd say: "I'm keeping it for best." I could feel her in the room and I didn't feel sad. I was going to tell Mom later but I didn't. I don't know why really.

Remember: Remembering is comforting

December 2nd

I slept like a log last night – first time in ages. I feel like going to the bike track with Stu and Lee today. It's chilly but I think the fresh air and being with my mates might help me.

Joy's Mom has invited us to their house for Christmas dinner this year. Me and Joy and Joy's grandad are making the mince pies. Joy's grandad lives with them since his wife died a long time ago. I don't know him very well but he waves to us when he's going to get a newspaper and we're on the way to school.

I think it's a good idea that we're not at home this Christmas because it will be too hard without Nan.

We put the tree up tonight and Mom showed me a new glass bauble she'd bought to put on the tree for Nan. It has glittery silver snowflakes on the outside and a small white feather inside. It hangs on a lilac ribbon with the word Love stitched into it.

I like it and Mom let me put it where I wanted to on the tree. I chose right in the centre where it's surrounded by silver bells and purple velvet bows. Nan would have liked that.

Remember: Get a special bauble at Christmas for someone you've loved and lost

Christmas Eve

I'm so angry and I'm not supposed to be because it's Christmas Eve. It's just not fair that other people have all their family together and I haven't! I plod downstairs and meet Mom in the kitchen. "What's wrong with your face? It's nearly Christmas!" "I'm angry, Mom," "What about?" "Everything. This isn't how it's supposed to be this close to Christmas." "Come and sit down, Danny, we need to talk. I know what this is about and I understand how you feel cos I feel like that too." "Do you Mom? I didn't realise." "I know, Danny, because I'm trying to be strong for you. That's why I don't talk about Nan very often. But I think about her every day." "I didn't realise, Mom," I said again.

I hadn't thought how hard it must be for her not to have either of her parents now. Can a grown-up be an orphan? I felt like opening up. "I don't talk about Nan cos I don't want to upset you." "I'm upset whether you talk to me about her or not, Danny. I think we both need to talk more." "Me too, Mom," I said. Mom gave me half a smile. "I've got an idea that will help you get rid of your anger. Let's go and pound some dough and make some bread to put in the freezer for Christmas. That always works for me."

"You never told me that, Mom." "I don't tell you everything, Danny."

In the kitchen Mom said "Let's listen to music while we're baking." I grabbed my Bob Marley CDs from the lounge and put my favourite one in the CD-player by the kettle and pressed play. We did loads of pounding, made some loaves and we both felt better. Music and baking go together for me now.

Remember: Music can make you feel calm

Christmas Day
Unexpectedly we had a good day despite the past few weeks. The food was great. Joy's mom is a good cook. Our mince pies went down a treat. We played Charades and Guess Who I Am and we all had a laugh.

Back at ours Mom went to make a cup of tea. I'd just switched on the TV when she called out: "Danny, put your coat on and come out here!" I said: "It's cold Mom, what is it?" "Just come, Danny, you'll see!" Off I went. She was standing in the garden. "Look up!" I looked up. The sky was black and my breath was making clouds in the chill night air. "What, Mom?" "Look! There, Danny! It's Nan! She's looking down on us!" I looked up again and there was one single, perfect star right above us shining brightly. She grabbed my hand and held it tightly. A tear rolled down her cheek. She quickly brushed it away but I saw it. I squeezed her hand tighter.

I couldn't say anything. We stood there in silence for a few minutes and then she said: "We love you to the moon and back," to the star and then we went back inside for hot chocolate.

Remember: Find your special star

January 12th
Would have been Nan's birthday today so we lit a candle by her photo and bought a bunch of pink roses to put in a vase next to it.

Joy's grandad came round and asked if I'd like to help him build a bird-table. I think Mr. Rose feels sorry for me cos of Nan. Joy says he's very kind. I said yes as I hadn't got anything else to do. I've never done any woodwork before so I've got no idea how it will turn out. I asked Joy if she wanted to come and help but she said "No thanks. It's not my thing." I didn't know if it was my thing either, but I'd give it a go.

Mr. Rose said: "Call me Derek if you like, Danny." He's got a kind face, tanned from the outdoors, deep brown eyes that twinkle and a gentle smile. We went up the path covered with a layer of crisp frost. A chubby little robin flew onto a bush on the left, stared right at me and flew off. Derek said: "That's my wife! She's always popping into the garden to check up on me." I said: "How do you know?" He smiled, looked me straight in the eye and said: "I _know_. And you'll see one soon. That'll be your Nan checking up on you."

He was so convincing, I believed him. "Does it make you sad?" I asked him. "No, lad, it's nice to know she's still around. Anyway, let's get in the shed and start our project." The shed smelt of wood, glue and paint – a proper manly smell. It was big inside and all the tools were neatly on hooks in rows. "Every man needs a man cave, his own space. Remember that, Danny, when you grow up." Soon I was sawing, chopping, nailing and gluing with Derek's help. He is patient and a good teacher. I learnt a lot and surprisingly enjoyed it.

Felt a bit guilty too, as for a while I'd forgotten about Nan and how sad I was. Then I remembered what Mom had said: "Nan wouldn't want us to be sad, Danny." I decided it was a bit soon for happy times though. Derek said: "Come back and we'll carry on whenever you want to, lad."

Remember: Don't feel guilty if you forget to be sad

Pancake Day

It's Pancake Day and Joy, her mom and Derek are coming round to eat with us. It's been snowing all day and very cold. The winter drags on.

I'm missing playing basketball with my mates Stu and Lee so am going to meet them at the basketball court later. We prefer to play outside but will have to settle for indoors today. The warm days spent at the Lickey

Hills seem far away at the moment.

Anyway the pancakes were great. We had fruit and ice-cream with them and we all ate far too many. Mom said: "Remember, Danny, how much Nan loved pancakes?" "I do, Mom. She always said you made the best in the world." We both had a moment.

Derek said: "Danny, we need to get on with the bird-table soon. The birds need something to have their food on in winter." "How about the weekend?" I said. "That would be great, lad."

Mother's Day

Got Mom a bunch of pink and purple flowers and a card for today. Knew it would be a difficult day for her: her first without her Mom. Took her tea and toast in bed. She was so surprised. Gave her the flowers and card. The verse made her cry.

I opened the curtains and noticed little green shoots appearing in the garden pots. We'd planted some snowdrops together last autumn. Spring was on its way again. Nan loved spring as well as autumn. Snowdrops were her favourite spring flowers. "Come and look, Mom," I said, and we stood at the window. Mom said: "Spring always makes me feel hopeful."

Easter

Derek and Joy's Mom had organised an Easter egg hunt in their garden. Me and Joy love chocolate so we were hoping we could work out all the clues and find all the eggs. Joy is quite competitive and bet me she'd find more eggs than me. I said: "Just you try!" The clues were a bit tricky but together we worked them out. We found eggs in plant pots, under bushes and in the shed amongst the tools. The best hiding-place was under a pile of bird food on their bird-table! Good job the chocolate eggs were wrapped up! If the squirrels found them first, bet they'd have a job getting the wrappers off!

The bird-table looks great in the garden and the birds must love it as they're always on it, feeding. Derek and I are making one for our garden next, as Mom would love it. I never knew I'd enjoy making them. I've grown to love the sanding part best. I like the sound it makes, and making something rough smooth. It's very satisfying.

I saw a robin today. Not the one I saw with Derek. It was smaller and fluffier. I like to think Nan was watching the Easter egg hunt. I'd never really looked properly at a robin before. They're so interesting.

May 17th

Saturday was wet and windy. When I came back from basketball Mom and I went shopping. She said: "Let's choose a really pretty album and we can take it home and fill it full of photos of us and Nan. Would you like that?" I thought for a moment. I wasn't quite sure how it would make me feel. "Yeah, I'd like that," I said.

Mom let me choose the album so I chose a large purple one with silver stars on, Nan's favourite colour. It's Mom's favourite colour too. "She'd have loved that, wouldn't she, Mom?" "She certainly would, Danny! Good choice!" At home we got out the flowery box full of photos from when I was born up to now. I chose my favourites and so did Mom. We took it in turns writing underneath them. Some were funny and some made Mom go: "Aah! That's sweet!".

I thought it would be a sad thing to do and we did have a little cry together at some, but mostly we smiled, laughed and just remembered. Mom said I could keep the album in my room, so I have. Remember: Happy memories are forever

June 1st

Mom's decided it's time for Patch's annual bath. This is always really strange because we never mention the word 'bath' and yet when we call her upstairs, which isn't unusual, she doesn't want to come. She sits at the bottom of the stairs looking at us reluctantly.

I end up going back down the stairs and pushing her up, as Mom calls from the top. I have to get into my swimming trunks and get in the bath and Mom lifts Patch into the water. Mom kneels at the side of the bath and we both shampoo and rinse her. I have to hang on for dear life as she tries to escape every few seconds. When we're done Mom has to hang onto her while I climb out, then we both hang onto her while we reach for the towels. Every time, as well as today, in the seconds it takes for us to reach for the towels, she escapes from us and shakes herself so Mom and I end up dripping with water and laughing! Glad we don't do this very often. What a drama!

June 6th

Derek's offered to show me his old car that he's doing up. I've always been into cars and how they work so this should be good. In the garage he showed me his old Cortina. He told me what it was as I had never seen a car like it before. Looks really old and in need of a new coat of paint.

He explained there was a long way to go before that happened. He told me about the stages of repair like getting the rust off, filling and priming. He said it was a big project he'd been doing for a few years already. As I followed his instructions we chatted happily. He is easy company, a good talker and a good listener too. He asked me about school. I said: "Don't really enjoy it.

Too much writing and not enough practical lessons." "Know what you mean, lad, I was the same." I said: "I worry that if I don't do well at secondary school it will be hard to get a job." "You don't want to be worrying about that now," he said, "That's years off! Anyway, I didn't do that well at school but still had a successful business as a mechanic. This world needs practical people as well. You're a bright lad. You'll make your own way when you find out what it is you want to do." "I think I'd to work with cars, cos I like them," I told him, "I've always wanted to. "Well, lad, I'd better teach you all I know because it could come in handy." We worked on the car for a few hours. Then I went home for tea. As I went up the path to my front door a feather landed in front of me. Wonder where that came from? I don't know but it made me feel good. Couldn't wait to tell Mom about what I've been doing, what Derek said and that feather. Mom's always telling me to look for signs and I think maybe that was one!

Remember: Find your own way

July 22nd

It's my birthday today. It wasn't the same this year cos there was no card or present off Nan, but Mom kept up the tradition of hiding my presents and playing Hot and Cold to find them. I've told her before I'm too big to play this game but she just does it anyway. I think she enjoys it even more than I do.

Found the basketball in the fridge, found the new trainers in the washing-machine, a rucksack in the oven, and - big surprise! - there was a new bike in the outhouse. Wow! Wasn't expecting that! It's black with orange racing stripes. Fantastic! Mom took me by surprise by telling me that Nan gave her some money just for me to buy the bike with. We hugged each other and shed a tear. We didn't say anything but both of us knew what we meant.

Having a party later. Stu and Lee are coming but I rang them to get here earlier, to see my new bike and go for a ride. Off we went. Nearly got to the bike track when I got a puncture! Had to phone Mom to come and pick me up in the car and put the bike in the back so I could come home and mend the puncture. What a pain! Didn't take me too long and I was soon back on the road. We had a great time.

Mom and I are putting up lights in the garden. I've got my mates and next door coming and Mom's friends are popping round as well. I'm sorting the music – lots of reggae, my favourite. Stu and Lee are bringing some music too.

It's great having a July birthday as it's light outside till late. Have suggested to Mom that she doesn't hang around with us outside all night and she said: "I don't intend to! I'll be chatting inside to my friends once I've done the food."

We all had such a laugh, me and my friends. It was a great party! Mom and I cleared up after they'd all gone. Just before we went in we both looked up, saw our star and smiled.

Remember: The best times are with family and friends

August 3rd

It was Saturday morning and Joy was knocking at the door. "Hi! You busy?" "No," I said, "Come on in." She was carrying a bag and I wondered what was inside.

She said hi to my Mom and let's go in the garden, I have something to show you. Mysterious! She pulled out a blue wooden box covered with star stickers. "I did this when my Nanny died and I want to show you."

She lifted the hinged top and showed me what was in there: an earring, a bracelet, a photo of her and her Nan, some shells, a small bottle of perfume and a feather. She said it was a memory box. I'd never heard of that. It was her mom's idea. She kept it in her bedroom. "Thought you might like to do one for your Nan," she said, "I get it out when I feel like it and just remember the happy times." Joy is so thoughtful. I said: "I like that idea, thanks." Joy said: "I got you a plain wooden box like mine. You could paint it and decorate it and then put in whatever you want. We could do it together if you like." I did want to, as I felt she understood. Anyway, my Nan really liked Joy. They often chatted together over the garden fence.

I started to think what I'd like to put inside. Shells – yes, from our last holiday. Perfume too – I liked that idea. In the kitchen there was a packet of forget-me-not seeds Nan and I were going to plant and didn't, so they could go in too. Jewellery – yes, that was a good idea too. Photos, definitely.

Nan had a tiny robin ornament. That would fit in too. I thought I knew where it was, but it wasn't there when I went to look. I shouted to Mom: "Where's Nan's robin? I can't find it!" She said: "I can't remember but I'll look for it later." Crossly I shouted: "But I need it now, Mom!" "I can't look for it now, Danny. I'm in the middle of paperwork. Soon as I've finished I'll look for it." "Leave it for now," Joy said, "We've got everything else." "But we have to have the robin cos it was Nan's favourite ornament," I said. I felt like I didn't want to do it now cos it wasn't going to be complete.

Just then Patch came into the garden and laid her head on my knee and looked up at me. Joy looked at me and said: "Danny, why don't we take Patch to the park and your Mom will probably have found the robin by the time we get back and we can do the box all in one go. I'll have Patch if you want to go on your bike."

The park was a great idea. When we got back Mom was in the kitchen and the robin was on the table. "Thanks for finding the robin, Mom," I said, "And sorry." "It's OK, it's forgotten. There's sandwiches and squash in the garden for you both."

Joy and I started painting the box. Purple, of course. It soon dried. Joy had brought stickers and I chose robins to put on. We gathered the things to go inside and sat back to admire the result. It was brilliant. Joy said "Because your Nan liked flowers, why don't you plant half the forget-me-not seeds and just keep the other half in the box?" "That's a great idea, Joy. I hadn't thought of that." I found an empty plant pot in the garden and Joy and I planted the seeds. We left them in a sunny spot by the back door. We showed Mom the box and she said: "Joy, that was a great idea, so thoughtful. That's a very special box. You've put such lovely memories in there, Danny. Come on, group hug!" "Oh Mom!" I said and smiled.

Remember: Best friends stick together

August 17th
We're off to Jersey today – us and next door! Will be brilliant! Joy hasn't flown before but Derek says he'll

hold her hand the whole way. It's only an hour's flight anyway. We haven't left Patch before but she'll be OK cos she's going to stay with Stu and Lee and she knows them really well. We will miss her but we're looking forward to the break.

Mom's rented a big cottage for us all near the beach. Must remember my bucket and net so Joy and me can go crabbing in the rock pools. Yeah! We're here and the sun is shining! We drop off our bags and head for the beach. Blue sea, golden sand and bright sun. Love it!

Joy and I clamber up the rocks to find the little pools hidden in the dips. Lots of tiny crabs are waiting for us. We catch loads and go to show them all. Derek said: "I loved that when I was a child. Come on, let's look for more." Off we went again leaving the moms to chat as usual. Derek turned out to be really good at it too. "You never forget!" he said, smiling. We put them all back near the end of the afternoon and started on building a sandcastle with a moat.

Everyone joined in and it looked brilliant when we'd finished. Mom had collected some seagull feathers and we stuck them on the top of the sandcastle. Mom took photos of us all and the sandcastle. "That's one for the album!" she said. She looked happy. "Nan would have loved it here," I said. "I know, love, I like to think she's looking down on us." "Me too," I said quietly.

Me and Joy are going to try kayaking and archery while we're here. It's good to do things with your friends, not just with the adults around.
Remember: You can be happy again

September 2nd

Start of a new term in a new school. We made the most of yesterday. Me and Joy, Stu and Lee spent most of the day at the bike track with a picnic. Nan usually bought my school uniform for me in the holidays but not this time. Patch had a good old sniff of my uniform. She knew something was different.

Both moms took photos of me and Joy before we set off. "It's for the album," Mom said, "It's a big day!" She was getting emotional so Joy and I left quickly. I wasn't nervous about going cos all my friends were going too. Did wonder what all the teachers would be like, but suppose if there's any you don't like, you don't spend all day with them like in Juniors. We met up with our mates in the playground. So many smart uniforms and new haircuts! Couldn't believe the size of the older kids and how many of them there were. Mind you, the building and playground are massive compared to our old school.

Wheelers' High is a popular school and the one most of us wanted to get into. We were lucky we were all starting together. The bell rang. Off we went, loads of us piling through the double doors. It's a new beginning for me and my friends. I've already signed up for karate club and basketball club and I'm thinking about joining Scouts at the local hall.

Remember: Life moves on

October 29th

It's Mom's birthday today. Been saving my pocket money to get a card and a climbing rose for the garden. She'll like that. I know she'll cry cos I got one called 'Mother's Love'. Derek and Joy took me to choose it at the garden centre. They know me there as Mom is often there buying compost, plants and pots. She loves her garden.

I sit out with her sometimes in the summer and we chat, but the planting and the weeding aren't my thing. She loved the rose. She cried of course, and then I helped her plant it. She's put it near the forget-me-not pot. Hope Patch doesn't go and dig it up! Joy, her mom, Derek and us two all went to the Red Lion for a meal. The puds were the best!

Remember: Mark the special days

November 5th: Bonfire Night

One of our big nights. We're having a bonfire, fireworks and food in the garden with next door. We always have jacket potatoes and home-made soup. Mom scoops out the cooked potato, mixes it with corned beef and butter and puts it back in the oven. Everyone loves those. Our favourite soup is vegetable.

Can't wait for it to get dark for it all to begin. Thank goodness it's not raining. The smell of damp leaves and burning smoke, with the fireworks that light up the night sky, make the perfect bonfire night. I know I'm eleven but Joy and I love to write our names in the air with the sparklers. I wouldn't tell my mates at school though. We don't have bangers because Patch gets scared. She'll spend the night under the dining-table in her basket with the TV on to drown out the noise of the fireworks.

The bonfire is huge! We collected wood that Derek had left over from one of his many projects. The food was delicious. We ate the potatoes with our gloves on to keep our hands warm. The stunning colours of the fireworks are still magical to me. I love the way they light up the night sky. Joy says they look like jewels.

I think Mom and I are alike cos she's always told me fireworks are magical. The night wasn't long enough for me. Now I'll have to wait another year to have this all again.

Remember: Real magic never fades

November 19th

One year today since we lost Nan. It's been a rollercoaster year of ups and downs. It's been hard but Mom and I have got through it together. We went to the garden centre and bought a small stone angel and two little metal robins for the garden. We wanted to do something special today. The second robin was for my Poppa.

When we got back we went into the garden to decide where to put them. Mom decided to put them next to the rose and the pot. She's moved the bench there for somewhere to sit and think. She was very quiet when we went back inside. She looked like she was going to cry. "I know today's hard, Mom. Please don't get upset." "I'm sorry Danny, I was just thinking about my dad. I still miss him even though it was years ago. I wanted him to see you grow up, be at your wedding and enjoy grandchildren." "I know Mom, I miss him too."

We spent so much time together it's left a huge hole in both of our lives. Her and Poppa were so close. They talked all the time and we were round a lot at their house. He was kind and generous and thought the world of me and Mom. He was always there to help us and Mom used to call him her rock. It was tough for her when it happened. She was sad for a long time. I was as well. She said today had reminded her about him too. Getting the robin for him had started her thinking. "Loss is never easy, Danny. You never stop missing them, but you learn to live with it." Why can't we all live forever, I wondered.

We chatted about the big house in Tenbury Road where they'd lived before Poppa went. It had an enormous garden where I spent a lot of time with him and Patch. We'd play out there, and even when I was little I used to help to water the garden. I have lots of photos from that time. Summers were always spent out there together. Their garden took up a lot of time with weeding, pruning and planting, but they both enjoyed it. Their garden had a big swing in and tall trees at the top. That's where Mom got her love of gardening from.

Although our garden is much smaller, I had lots of fun. Had a sandpit out there which I used to play in for hours, and I made a zip-line from my bedroom window to the sandpit for Action Man to go down. Brilliant! There was a low picket fence to the left and whenever I was out there the old couple next door, Les and Flo, would come out and give me pennies for my money box. Mom told me once that they didn't have much, but they were still generous. They've gone now, but I've never forgotten.

Mom told me when she was young there was a

summer-house in the big garden too. I wish it had still been there when I was younger. She said it was a proper little house with a piano, chairs, a table and carpet. That would have made a brilliant man cave!

I had my own bedroom at Nan and Poppa's too, where I stayed when Mom was at work. Once Poppa had gone, the house and garden were too big for Nan to manage so she came to live with us.

Mom seemed a bit better after we'd chatted. She said: "Danny, why don't you go down the bike track with Stu and Lee?" "Yeah, I'd like to Mom - will you be OK?" "I'll be fine," she said, "Joy's mom's coming round in a while for a catch-up. We can watch that elephant documentary with David Attenborough later, if you like."

Elephants are Mom's favourite animal. She says it's because they can show emotion. A lot like Mom! Anyway, I felt OK going out cos I knew she wasn't going to be on her own.

On my way to Stu and Lee's a feather landed on my handlebars. I'm beginning to think what Mom says about signs might be true, after all. I just felt we'd be

OK. Don't really know why.

Remember: anniversaries can be hard – that's normal

December 14th

Christmas is just around the corner. It will be easier this year as next door and us are going back to Jersey, to the Somerville Hotel at St. Ouens Bay. Mom and I love it there. It's on a hill overlooking the harbour. From there you can see all the way round the coast as far as St. Helier. You can see the boats and hear the anchor chains clanking at night when it's quiet. It's a really handy place to stay cos you can walk down the hill to the harbour and there's a lot of different places to eat. A different one every night if you want.

Next door haven't been to the hotel before. We can show them all our favourite places they haven't been yet, like the Lookout beach café on the seafront at St. Helier. We spent so much time on the beaches last time that we didn't get chance to show them everything.

We enjoyed kayaking last time, but you can't do it in winter cos the sea gets rough. We enjoyed archery as well and are going to do that again. We must go to the zoo cos Joy's really into conservation. Joy and I have read all of Gerald Durrell's books. In fact she got me into them. His zoo is his legacy, Mom says. Before we go Mom and I will go and choose a new bauble for Nan. Mom's packing a little Christmas tree and the new bauble, and the one from last Christmas. We'll put the tree up in our hotel room when we get there. It'll be like taking Nan with us.

From nowhere, a robin landed on the windowsill.

The End

Things that helped Danny:
Talk to family and friends about how you feel
Know it's normal to feel sad – it takes time

Spend time alone if you need to
Find an activity you enjoy to lose yourself in
Play the music that calms you
Mark special dates e.g. plant something or buy
    something that reminds you
Take a walk or a bike ride
Spend time with a pet
Fill a photo album
Make a memory box
Find your star
Watch out for robins, feathers and other signs

We never completely lose those that have gone.
They are part of us and we are part of them.
Because they will always live on in us, as a comfort
and a guide, in time we can be happy again.

© Susan Jayne Rose MMXVIII